LANDSCAPES ON DERBY AND WORCESTER PORCELAIN

LANDSCAPES ON
DERBY AND WORCESTER PORCELAIN

by
John Twitchett
and Henry Sandon

Foreword by Ian T. Henderson
Introduction by A. W. Coysh

Henderson and Stirk Ltd
Publishers

First edition 1984
Published by Henderson and Stirk Ltd
c/o Routledge/Harrap Storage Ltd
Broadway House
Newton Road
Henley on Thames, Oxon RG9 1EN

ISBN 0 9506549 5 7

Consultant publishers
Lund Humphries Publishers Ltd
26 Litchfield Street, London WC2

Made and printed in Great Britain by
BAS Printers Limited
Over Wallop, Hampshire

Contents

List of Illustrations

Foreword

Having built up a collection of topographical ceramics over the years, my wife and I have sponsored a series of books which describe the landscapes to be found on pottery and porcelain. These include:

Pictorial Souvenirs of Britain, Ian T. Henderson

Pictorial Souvenirs and Commemoratives of North America, Frank Stefano, Jr

Collecting Ceramic Landscapes, A. W. Coysh and Frank Stefano, Jr

We are now delighted to complete the sequence by publishing *Landscapes on Derby and Worcester Porcelain*, illustrated mainly with pieces from our own collection. The artists who painted these landscapes have long been neglected. John Twitchett and Henry Sandon are experts in this field, well qualified to describe their work.

I have always found the scenes on ceramics fascinating and with the help once more of Mr A. W. Coysh, who has written an introduction, the historical significance of the scenes themselves can now be more fully appreciated.

Ian T. Henderson

The Cult of the Picturesque
by A. W. Coysh

Many of our museums and country houses display collections of fine British porcelain dating from the late eighteenth century, often superbly decorated with miniature landscapes. What made the manufacturers abandon the traditional oriental designs which had previously been used on porcelain and turn to this refreshingly new style of decoration? Several factors combined to bring about this change.

Interest in British scenery was largely stimulated by one man, the Rev. William Gilpin (1724–1804). He was a landscape artist who focused attention on natural scenery which he described as 'picturesque', a description which soon came to be widely accepted. He made sketching tours in East Anglia, the Wye Valley, South Wales, the South of England, the Lake District and the Highlands of Scotland, publishing a series of books illustrated with his own pen drawings. His first book, *Observations on the River Wye*, published in 1782, was an immense success and Gilpin's picturesque 'rules of beauty', stressing the simplicity and grandeur of nature, exerted a profound influence on taste. As a result many people who had previously thought only in terms of the Grand Tour of Europe began to explore Britain. A flood of travel books followed and by the turn of the century the 'Picturesque Road Map' appeared with sketches of the scenes travellers could expect to see from their coach or post-chaise.

There were, however, other influences at work. Many fine country mansions were built in the eighteenth century and Lancelot Brown (1748–1793), better known as Capability Brown, was commissioned by many owners to create landscapes of lakes, lawns and woodland around their properties to which they were only too glad to welcome respectable admiring visitors. Brown's work was scorned by Gilpin and his disciples. Payne Knight refers to mansions 'fresh from th'improvers desolating hand' and to Brown as the 'thin, meagre genius of the bare and bald'. Gilpin's ideas, however, were also under criticism, though mainly in humorous vein. In 1820 William Coombe published a series of doggerel verses in book form, illustrated by Thomas Rowlandson, under the title *The Tour of Dr Syntax in Search of the Picturesque.* These lampooned Gilpin, thinly disguised as Dr Syntax, so successfully that other books followed. The controversy proved to be wonderful publicity for British tourism.

Many books appeared with views of the seats of the 'Noblemen and Gentlemen', notably volumes by Jones & Co. and by J. P. Neale. The work of the architect, John Nash (1752–1835) around Regent's Park in London was also illustrated in a series of drawings by Thomas Shepherd in *Metropolitan Improvements* (1827).

Engravings from many books on scenery and country mansions were widely copied not only on porcelain but also as transfer prints on pottery and Scottish woodware. The landscapes on porcelain appeared on vases and on tea and dinner services though some of the finest are found on the rarer dessert services used for the tropical fruits which were grown in country house orangeries. Most services were specially commissioned. Some were decorated with views of the owners' estates or with views to remind them of places visited on a tour. Alternatively they could choose from lists of the great houses with the names of their owners provided by the porcelain manufacturers or retailers.

Although many of the landscapes were copied from engravings, some of the ceramic artists made their own sketches in the field. It was a highly skilled craft for not only had many of the landscapes to be painted on curved surfaces but allowances had to be made for changes of colour in the heat of a kiln.

Pre-eminent among the porcelain factories producing landscape wares were those at Derby and Worcester. Unfortunately, the Derby artists did not sign their work until early in the nineteenth century and the Worcester artists even later. However, a good deal is known about the artists in both centres and this book describes their work and illustrates some of the landscapes they painted.

The Landscape Painters of Derby

by John Twitchett FRSA

The Three Factories

Landscape painting in the topographical sense was first used in the Derby factory in England in the third quarter of the eighteenth century, taking full advantage of the beautiful surrounding Derbyshire countryside. This form of decoration appeared on services for tea, dinner and dessert as well as ornamental wares. Landscape painting on Derby porcelain became very popular and, to some extent, competed with the natural floral style for which the factory was so celebrated.

To understand the development of landscape painting at Derby it is necessary to know something of the history of the works. About the year 1748 Andrew Planché, a young man of Huguenot descent, was thought to be the first man to make porcelain in Derby. There are known to be some small jugs, one of which is marked 'Derby 1750'. By word of mouth it has been passed down that Planché lived in Lodge Lane, Derby and in a document drawn up in 1756 Andrew Planché, John Heath (Banker) and the first William Duesbury are all mentioned. They agreed to become co-partners 'in ye Art of making English China as also in buying and selling of all sorts of wares belonging to ye Art of making China . . .'.

In this agreement Planché is described as of Derby and 'China Maker'. William Duesbury, later to play such an important role in the Derby story, is named as 'Wm. Duesbury of Longton in ye County of Stafford Enamellor'.

The copy of the 'Articles of Agreement' which was found was not signed and in fact Planché's name does not again appear officially. He did however leave behind a range of figures known as 'dry edge' – figures which are amongst the finest English porcelain figures ever modelled.

It was, however, Duesbury who later expanded production at the Derby factory in Nottingham Road and before his death he had raised it to a position of pre-eminence in the land. Later, his son, William Duesbury II, gathered around himself a remarkable group of painters including Zachariah Boreman, George Complin, William Billingsley, Richard Askew, James Banford, and John Brewer, as well as modellers Stephan, Spangler, Hardenburg and William Coffee.

During the last years of the eighteenth century Duesbury II took into partnership Michael Kean, an Irish miniature painter. After Duesbury II's death in 1797, his widow married Kean who continued to manage the works. However, family troubles shattered the great manufactory and, although the business was carried on as 'Duesbury and Kean', Duesbury III never played an active role in the business.

In 1809 the factory was advertised for sale and in 1811 the

lease was granted to Robert Bloor, a clerk at the factory. Unfortunately he did not have the artistic knowledge and experience of his predecessors but, during the early part of his control, many fine services and vases were produced. These showed the change in public taste; they were flamboyantly decorated with fruit, landscapes, bird, figure and floral subjects, reserved within heavily scrolled gilt borders. The workmanship was of the very highest order. Unfortunately, Bloor's health declined owing to his addiction to alcohol, probably brought on by the strain of financial worry and trade recessions. Eventually in about 1828 he became mentally unbalanced and from then onwards the production of quality goods declined and some of Derby's finest painters left to work in the Staffordshire Potteries or elsewhere. In 1848 the Nottingham Road works closed. Fortunately, this was not the end of porcelain manufacture in Derby. Six of the employees of the old Nottingham Road factory – William Lockyer, Samuel Fearn, John Henson, Samuel Sharpe, James Hill and Sampson Hancock – managed to set up a small factory in King Street. The original Duesbury potters' wheel and certain moulds and patterns were taken to King Street. The traditional Derby figures, Imari style decoration and other patterns were continued. The works even survived competition from its larger neighbour the Derby Crown Porcelain Company which was established at Osmaston Road, Derby in 1877 by Edward Phillips and William Litherland who had left the Royal Worcester Company. In 1935 the King Street concern was merged into this world-famous firm which had become The Royal Crown Derby Porcelain Company, providing a continuity of tradition and the opportunity to make valuable contributions to the ceramic world, which are continued in the name of Crown Derby.

The Landscape Painters

Landscape decoration on Derby Porcelain has been notable for some 200 years. From about 1785 until the closure of the Nottingham Road factory in 1848, this form of decoration extended its bounds to cover not only Britain but Europe as well. One frequently finds decorated ware with inscriptions such as 'In Italy', 'In Germany', or 'In Portugal' etc., written on the reverse side.

It is clear that although flower painting and the simple set motif composed the largest output of the factory, landscape painting was from the early 1780s always in demand until by the nineteenth century it had increased its share of the total output considerably. Decoration on Derby porcelain embraced all subjects from flowers to figures and its diversity must not be underestimated.

Most of the landscapes were based on contemporary prints from such publications as *Middiman's Views*, *Harrington's Engravings of the Lakes*, and *Hazle's Tour to the Isle of Wight*, but some painters obviously used sketch books as there are surviving examples at the Derby Museum and in private collections.

Like other porcelain manufactories of the period, painters did not sign their work, except early in the nineteenth century when they signed plaques, though it is worth noting that these were usually executed in their *own time*. Edward Prince was one of the first men to sign his work but this was after 1860 at the King Street works.

The Old Derby Pattern Books, used by the Duesbury family at Nottingham Road, have survived and are believed to be the only surviving patterns of an eighteenth-century porcelain manufactory in Britain. They have proved an invaluable aid to research (*Old Derby Pattern Books*, J. Twitchett, 1971). In the tea pattern book the numbers run up to 770 and in the dessert and dinner service book to just over 400. Much useful information about the painters has been extracted from them, as some have the name of a particular painter written on them.

There are, of course, dangers in trying to attribute named patterns. An artist may have left the factory or might be working on a more pressing order so another artist used to painting similar objects was sometimes given the work to complete. Occasionally, a large service might need several artists working to complete an order in good time. Take, for example, plate pattern No. 178 described as 'Landskip near Critch by Boreman'; not only must his style be reasonably attributable but the paste and glaze must also appear contemporary with the period of Boreman's stay at Derby from 1783–95 since later services of this pattern were painted by Hill, Robertson and the Brewer brothers.

The earliest number to have a topographical description is pattern No. 35; pattern no. 26 is a landscape plate painted in polychrome colours and although no painter is mentioned it is clearly the work of Zachariah Boreman. At that time the factory mark was usually in puce but where a description was written on the ware it was in blue. An exception was shown in the 1973 Exhibition of the products of the Nottingham Road factory (exhibit No. 13) inscribed in puce 'Grasmere', which was clearly the work of Boreman.

It is also possible to date from documentary evidence relating to the pattern numbers (see Lygo's letters to Duesbury – in the writer's *Derby Porcelain*, 1980). The latest puce marked piece so far recorded is a jug pattern No. 544 dated 1801, and it may be assumed that the tea patterns (770) were completed early in the nineteenth century (*c.* 1805) and remained in full use until Robert Bloor took over in 1811. It is also fair to suggest that the Derby mark did not change to the red mark generally until about 1807. The first printed marks were used about 1825 when it was decided that it took too long to paint the mark and some gilders were careless in executing this task. Until about 1835, when the printed Gothic Crown over 'D' was introduced, the mark had included the word 'Bloor'.

The following alphabetical list gives the names of Derby landscape painters, together with their approximate dates at the respective factories where they worked:

Ablott, Richard	1825–48	Nottingham Road
Askew, Richard	1772–80	Nottingham Road
	1794–98	
Banford, James	1789–95	Nottingham Road

Billingsley, William — Nottingham Road
It is necessary, in the light of modern research, to include this celebrated flower painter who whilst at Derby specialised in the painting of roses. Billingsley certainly did a good deal of landscape and figure painting whilst at Pinxton, Mansfield, Torksey and at Swansea, and possibly at Worcester, Nantgarw and Coalport. It is possible that this painter did do landscape painting at Derby, although it is the writer's opinion that it would have been strictly limited.

Boreman, Zachariah	1783–94	Nottingham Road
Brewer, John	1793–1816	Nottingham Road
Brewer, Robert	1797–1820	Nottingham Road
Clarke, Ellis,	1885–1901	Osmaston Road
Corden, William	1811–25	Nottingham Road
Cotton, William	1810–18	Nottingham Road
Crawley, Michael	1958–78	Osmaston Road
Dean, W. E. J.	1895–1950	Osmaston Road
Gresley, Cuthbert	1893–1955	Osmaston Road
Hancock, Harry Sampson	1895–1934	King Street
Hill, Thomas ('Jockey')	1795–1800	Nottingham Road
Holtzendorff, G.	1878–1887	Osmaston Road
Lucas, Daniel	1820–48	Nottingham Road
McLacklan	1805–10	Nottingham Road
Mosley, William E.	1893–1912	Osmaston Road
	1912–25	King Street
	1933–35	King Street
	1935–*c.* 1953	Osmaston Road
Mountford, Jesse	1815–1921	Nottingham Road

Nowacki, Stefan — Osmaston Road
One of the most talented painters in the ceramic world at the present time. He worked at the Royal Crown Derby works until the mid-1970s when he left to work as an independent decorator covering most subjects but particularly marine views.

Pratt, Henry Lark	1820–30	Nottingham Road
Prince, Edward	1830–48	Nottingham Road
	1849–70?	King Street
Randall, Thomas Martin	1795–1813	Nottingham Road

Like Billingsley this fine painter worked at Derby and it is the writer's firm belief that some fine landscape painting has yet to be identified.

Robertson, George	1797–1825	Nottingham Road
Rouse, James	1820–26	Nottingham Road
	1875–82	King Street
	1882–88	Osmaston Road

Statham, W. N.	1880–85	Osmaston Road
Trowell, Edwin	1882–1892	Osmaston Road
Wale, John Porter	1877–1919	Osmaston Road

It is worth noting the long period of service some of these landscape painters spent at the Derby factories.

The range of work by the Derby landscape painters over nearly 200 years is now illustrated by specific examples which trace the history of the art from the 1770s to the present day.

Nottingham Road Painters and Their Work

Zachariah Boreman

The most famous, and undoubtedly one of the finest, landscape painters was Zachariah Boreman, who had come to Derby in 1783 from Chelsea. His early work at Derby consisted of monochrome scenes, 'black upon moonlight', 'black upon fire' and, of course, coloured scenes. In the black upon moonlight, the details were painted in black upon a pale cream wash and similarly on orange for black upon fire. Boreman painted in subdued colours giving more attention to detail than colour, although his style changed after about 1790 when he tended to use more local colour, as in the Kedleston Vase.

Kedleston Hall was built during the years 1757–65 for Sir Nathaniel Curzon, first Baron Scarsdale, a great admirer of the architecture of ancient Rome. It is not surprising that after earlier disagreements in 1760, Robert Adam, who had recently returned from Italy was called in. Kedleston is considered by many to be the finest unspoilt example of the great architect's work. The Hall stands on the site of the original twelfth-century manor house and is famous for its marble hall and state rooms, which house many fine old masters, contemporary furniture and works of art. The Scarsdale family have long been patrons of the Derby porcelain works and only recently a new Kedleston Vase, which shows the South front of the Hall on one side and Viscount Scarsdale's coat of arms on the reverse, has been made by Royal Crown Derby. It is interesting to compare the style of Boreman's Kedleston Hall with that of the water-colour sketch of the same subject by another Derby artist, George Robertson.

Upon leaving Derby in 1794, Zachariah Boreman returned to London, working for Sims, who was one of the old Derby hands. It is not surprising, therefore, that some of his work for Sims has been mistaken for Derby. While at the Sims Studio, Boreman decorated much French china. The pair of plates illustrated with landscapes, which at first sight might appear to be Derby, are a good example. He continued to introduce small figures into his landscapes which are more often than not on the water's edge. The twin-arched bridge which can be seen in the Mill Dale scene is the Viator or Packhorse Bridge mentioned by Isaak Walton in *The Compleat Angler*, 1653. It is interesting to note that in 1787 the Derby factory purchased from a print seller, one Mr Byrne's 'Six Views all in Westmorland'.

The Kedleston Vase painted by Zachariah Boreman, c. 1790. Courtesy of the Royal Crown Derby Museum.

(opposite page)
Named views of Mill Dale, Derbyshire and Westmorland, painted on French porcelain by Zachariah Boreman.

Kedleston Hall
A watercolour sketch by George Robertson, 1796. Courtesy of Derby Museum and Art Gallery.

The Bemrose Can with named views in Dovedale, painted by Zachariah Boreman, c. 1790–97. Marks and descriptions in blue.

Zachariah Boreman died in Pimlico, London in February 1810, at the age of 72.

An exceptionally fine can and stand is painted with views of the Dove. One shows 'Tissington Spires', a famous rock formation in the valley of the river Dove and a mounted herdsman with his animals. The view on the other side of the can shows Thorpe Cloud and includes figures. Note the elegant figure with cane and dog. Such figures were, in fact, typical of Boreman's work. The subtle painting of the path and grasslands to the left of the picture are also characteristic.

William Bemrose, FSA, was a leading collector of fine art, who lived at Elmhurst, Derby and was head of the printing and publishing firm of Bemrose & Sons, a civic dignitary and collaborator with Alfred Wallis, then editor of the *Derby Mercury*, in producing the first authorative work on Derby porcelain – *The Pottery and Porcelain of Derbyshire*, 1870. This work was prepared for the Midland Counties Fine Arts and Industrial Exhibition, Derby in 1870. (The writer is fortunate in possessing the Wallis manuscript, together with unpublished details and paper cuttings.)

The can was offered as Lot 562 in the Bemrose Sale at Elmhurst in 1909. It was for many years the property of Anthony Hoyte, a well-known collector of Derby porcelain.

The tea cup painted with an oval landscape, shows Little Eaton, Derby. The pattern number is 131. The Derby tea pattern book, however, does not name a painter until pattern No. 220, painted by James Banford. In the opinion of the writer this cup is too early to attribute either to John Brewer or 'Jockey' Hill and although it could have been painted by Zachariah Boreman it is not painted in his normal style. Could we be looking at a genuine Banford landscape? It is true that the majority of his patterns, in all numbering sixteen, were figure subjects, but 220 may be a tinted landscape by Banford. Attributions have often been made rashly in the past without sufficient attention being paid to the colour of the marks or periods at which the painters are known to have worked at their respective factories.

The Brewer Brothers

When Zachariah Boreman left Derby in 1794 he was, at first, succeeded by John Brewer, who had arrived at Derby in late April 1793 (at least one year before 'Jockey' Hill's arrival). However, because Brewer was also a fine figure and animal painter, it is probable that he was engaged more in this type of decoration after Hill's arrival in 1794. The well-known water-colour artist, Paul Sandby RA (1725–1809), provided much inspiration for the Brewers and other early Derby landscape painters and this accounts for their style of painting. Robert Brewer, the younger Brewer brother, arrived at Derby about 1797, and painted landscapes for twenty-three years.

Little Eaton
A teacup possibly painted by James Banford. Pattern No. 131. Puce mark.

The view by John Brewer described as 'On the Dove' is not unusual, but it is worth noting that fishing never seems far from the painters' mind. Again a small figure is to be seen to the right hand of the picture! It must never be assumed, however, as

View in Dovedale
On a plate Pattern No. 148 by John Brewer, 1793–5. Mark and description in blue.

some assert, that because a figure is present in a landscape it is the work of a particular artist, such as Zachariah Boreman. It is important to distinguish the manner in which figures are painted and this is a great help in attributing work to a particular painter. Boreman's figures usually include rather elegantly dressed people, possibly showing a London influence since he had previously worked at Chelsea, and figures by Hill, Robertson and John Brewer are somewhat similar. Robert Brewer's figures, however, often appear to have rather ape-like faces, a characteristic which helps the collector to distinguish his work.

The view 'Dovedale' was painted by John Brewer whose use of the water-colour style helps greatly in attribution. The plate is marked and described in blue and is pattern No. 148. In the old Derby Pattern Books, pattern No. 139 was 'got up' for the Margrave of Ansbach and this important service was prepared in 1793 and was mentioned by Duesbury's London agent, Lygo, in his letter to his employer in 1793. Thus, it is fair to assume that pattern No. 148 was introduced in this year or certainly no later than the beginning of 1794. Hill, Robertson and Robert Brewer had not yet arrived in Derby and therefore Zachariah Boreman and John Brewer were the only landscape painters at the factory. This service is certainly not the work of Boreman, but this view of Dovedale is typical of John Brewer's pleasing water-colour style.

The Derwent and the Dove were always the favourite haunts of the Derby landscape painters and most of them were able to sketch views to add to the print views which were kept at the factory. One finds 'View in Dovedale' and 'On the River Derwent' (see opposite page) frequently painted on the landscape-decorated Derby porcelain.

Robert Brewer, younger brother of John Brewer, tended to darken his landscapes more than his brother and often used puce-colour undertones in his landscape painting. The Brewers were an artistic family whose parents had several studios in London. The Brewer brothers both exhibited. John showed 'Flies from Nature' at the Free Society of Artists in 1779, and 'Butterflies from Nature' in 1780. He was quite young and was addressed as 'Master Brewer'. Robert exhibited a 'View of Finchley Common' at the Royal Academy in 1797. Although it had been suggested that Robert was a more versatile artist than his brother, this would seem illogical as John's documented subjects include figures, flowers, landscapes, seascapes, birds and animals and, in the writer's opinion, military encampment scenes, whereas Robert is documented to have painted only landscapes and seascapes. The Brewers both became drawing masters in Derby.

Thomas ('Jockey') Hill

Thomas Hill, nicknamed 'Jockey' because he rode a pony to work, joined the Derby factory in 1794. He had been influenced, whilst working at Chelsea, by Zachariah Boreman and was, therefore, a water-colour artist. His work, however, lacks the subtle definition of Boreman's but usually includes more local

On the River Derwent
Painted by John Brewer on a teapot stand. Mark and description in red.

colour. Unfortunately, because of Hill's use of yellow in his landscapes, sometimes too dominant, his work is often confused with that of John Brewer or George Robertson who also used yellow a great deal. When making an attribution one must check that the paste, glaze and date are contemporary with the painter's period at the factory. Hill also exhibited at the Royal Academy.

Darley Grove has provided many generations of Derby townsfolk with a most beautiful walk along the banks of the Derwent and, of course, the Derby painters with much inspiration for their sketching. The subject plaque on page 23 was painted by 'Jockey' Hill for his great friend, a gentleman named Horsley, of Pye Bridge, Derbyshire and was eventually acquired by John Haslem, Derby artist, chronicler and miniature painter to Queen Victoria. A later view of Darley Grove is a sketch by Moses Webster who was a fine flower painter but was never considered a landscape artist.

George Robertson

Several painters joined the factory towards the end of the eighteenth century including Richard Askew and James Banford, who were the factory's chief figure painters but did, from time to time, execute landscapes. Much more important for landscape and shipping scenes was the arrival of George Robertson, whose work is always full of meticulous detail and fine colour, features which place him alongside Boreman as one of the finest of all Derby painters. A native of Ayrshire, Scotland, he married Ann Yates, daughter of one of Derby's best gilders, John Yates. It is not surprising that Robertson should have favoured Scottish scenes.

Robertson was very fond of using autumn colours and both these Scottish scenes show this to advantage. The tree in the foreground of the Forfar view on page 26 is painted in a similar style to the sketch of the elm tree on the same page which has been taken from George Robertson's own sketch book.

A framed porcelain plaque depicting another Derbyshire view – a good example of 'Jockey' Hill's style. Unmarked.

Darley Grove, Derby
Documentary Plaque painted by 'Jockey' Hill, 1795. Unmarked. Courtesy of Derby Museum and Art Gallery.

Sketch of Darley Grove by Moses Webster.

Views in Ireland and Scotland painted by George Robertson on yellow-ground coffee wares (above) and teacups (opposite). Pattern No. 531. Marks and descriptions in blue, c. 1797–1800.

It is interesting to note in the Derby pattern books that plate patterns Nos. 222, 245, 254, are all shipping scenes painted by Robertson and that 280 is a landscape. In the tea book, 406, 416, 417 and 418 are landscapes by Robertson.

We know rather more about Robertson than most Derby painters since three of his sketch books exist in the hands of private collectors and a series of his water-colour sketches, some of them signed, are in the Derby museum.

This cup, the left-hand view, shows the 'Salmon Leap near Dublin, Ireland'. This location is less than ten miles from the City. The Danish word 'Leixlip' means Salmon Leap and was adapted as the name. This particular leap has always been famous. It was formed by the River Liffey passing at great speed over a stretch of limestone rock in a broad smooth current. In 1949, however, a dam was constructed at this point and the leap has now been replaced by a 'fish-pass'. The right-hand view is 'Near Perth, Scotland'.

The left-hand teacup has a view 'On the Banks of the Clyde near Glasgow'. The centre cup is 'Near Yester, Scotland' and the right-hand cup 'On the River Clyde near Dumbarton, Scotland'. The colouring of all the scenes corresponds to that in the Robertson sketches. He appears to have been consistent in their use.

The documentary coffee-cup, although un-named, is clearly 'Dovedale Stepping Stones', painted by Edwin Trowell and made at Osmaston Road in 1888 (see page 27). It is based on

Hill's pattern No. 459 and indirectly it confirms the contrasting styles of Robertson and Hill.

The tureen (Colour Plate 2) shows a view of Matlock High Tor, Derbyshire, which compares with a Robertson sketch in the Derby Museum. It is, of course, a favourite of the Derby painters and has been used many times during the Nottingham Road, King Street and Osmaston Road periods.

The plates show views 'near Northallerton, Yorkshire', 'near Husworth, Durham', 'near Coupar in Fifeshire, Scotland', of 'Bala Lake, Merionethshire', 'on Merrow Common (Colour Plate 4), Surrey', and 'In the Isle of Wight', 'On the road to Deptford, Kent' (Colour Plate 3), and 'Llanwrst Bridge, Wales'. The Isle of Wight view is based on Plate 6 of Middiman's *Select Views in Great Britain* painted by J. Smith and engraved by S. Middiman, published 30 July 1784. A note to this picture says:

> 'The cliffs at Steephill, seen in this view, rise boldly from the beach. . . . The ride from Steephill to Shanklin Chine commands a full view of Sandown Bay. . . . The singularity of the situation at Steephill induced the late Mr Stanley, governor of the Island, to erect a cot upon the most romantic part, under the cliff'.

All the foregoing plates serve to illustrate the very great importance of Robertson's work to the collector and student alike and underlines the fact that his work is always full of

Reverse side of yellow ground teapot shown in Colour Plate 1, and (below) drawing of similar tree study from George Robertson's sketch book.

Dovedale Stepping Stones
Coffee-cup painted by Edwin Trowell, 1888. Crown Derby mark.

Four views painted by George Robertson on a lime-green dinner service, (c. 1800). Pattern No. 321. All with marks and descriptions in blue.

Near Husworth, Durham.

Llanwrst Bridge, Wales.

Bala Lake, Merionethshire.

Isle of Wight, Hampshire.

meticulous detail. This is all the more remarkable when one considers the difficulties involved in ceramic painting, including the inevitable change of the colours during the successive firings.

Ornamental plant pots and stands were produced in reasonably large quantities and rank with vases as amongst the most highly rated wares. Their function was to hide the unsightly earthenware pots which held the plants and to provide water for the plants through a small circular hole in the centre of the base, the small stands having been filled with water. Such shapes afforded equally good 'canvasses' for floral, figure, fruit, bird or indeed any decoration.

The 'Besborough' scene in County Kilkenny and the Welsh scenes depicting 'Pont-y-Glyn-Dyffwys, Corwen, Merioneth', (Colour Plate 5) once again show Robertson's great liking for autumn colours.

When Robertson left the Derby factory about 1820 he, like the Brewers, became an art master in the town. Later he went to Nottingham where, sadly, he died in a lunatic asylum.

McLacklan
This artist was employed by Derby during the early years of the nineteenth century, painting landscapes mainly in monochrome. Unfortunately, few documented pieces by McLacklan exist, so caution should be observed in attributing this artist's work.

Nottingham Road in the Bloor Period

Some early Derby landscape painters continued to work for the firm when Robert Bloor took over in 1811 but did not survive to the end of his tenure. Jesse Mountford, who had painted landscapes, was discharged by Bloor in 1821 together with three flower painters. It has been suggested that his style resembled that of a theatrical scenic artist. In the meantime such painters as William Cotton (1810–18) and William Corden (1815–25) joined the firm, both regarded as good landscape artists.

William Corden
A landscape painter who later distinguished himself by obtaining the patronage of William IV, Queen Victoria and the Prince Consort for portrait subjects.

William Cotton
The mug with the picture of Pickford's Fly Wagon (Colour Plate 7), attributed to William Cotton, is an unusual and striking subject. He was noted for painting scenes in the hunting field.

The firm of Pickfords was established over three hundred years ago in the North Midlands. During the reign of Charles II, Thomas Pickford started a packhorse business to haul stones needed for road mending. The Pickford van shown here was known as a 'Fly Wagon' used for fast delivery service in the 1780s between the places named on the vehicle – Leeds, Sheffield, Nottingham, Liverpool, Manchester and London.

Until the middle of the nineteenth century, artists depicted horses travelling at speed with their fore and hind legs stretched out. The advent of photography revealed the error and artists later showed the correct movements.

It is interesting to note that William Cotton has painted the tower of All Saints' Cathedral, Derby, in the background – as he did in various other local views. Indeed, its inclusion in his landscapes appears to have been almost the equivalent of a signature.

Daniel Lucas

By 1820 Daniel Lucas had arrived from the Davenport factory and had begun to establish himself in the role of chief landscape painter at Derby. Unlike the water-colour style of the earlier artists, Lucas's style was that of the oil painter and tended to be subdued in colouring though one must remember that the later painters had to contend with a difficult body and glaze.

Rivaulx Abbey was founded in 1131 and Walter Espee, who founded Kirkham Abbey, became the first Abbot. The abbey church is built north and south owing to the lie of the land which slopes towards the River Rye. The ruined transepts have

Rivaulx Abbey, Yorkshire
Porter mug, with a reserve painted by Daniel Lucas, c. 1820. Mark and description in red.

Norman work but the choir is Early English. This great abbey, in the Yorkshire Dales, was one of the largest early Cistercian church buildings in England.

The painted landscape by Daniel Lucas on a bough pot illustrates his skilful use of light (Colour Plate 8). Willersley Castle, Cromford, now used as a Methodist holiday centre, was built by William Thomas of London, for Sir Richard Arkwright, in 1782–88. The interior was burnt out three years later and had to be redone.

In the Preston area goods of linen mixed with cotton were manufactured on a considerable scale and as Arkwright watched the various processes early in his life, his thoughts turned to possible improvements in the mode of spinning, though it was some years before he realised his ambition. He was a barber by trade, but about 1767 he left his business at Wirksworth and went around the country buying hair. Arriving in Warrington, he designed a mechanism for a kind of perpetual motion. A clockmaker, named John Kay, suggested that this would be better used for an engine for cotton spinning. Kay and Arkwright then applied to Peter Atherton, of Liverpool, for some assistance in building such an engine. After some doubts, Atherton agreed and in this way the first Arkwright engine was made. After failure at Nottingham, owing to high production costs, two larger mills powered by water were erected at Cromford; the first in 1771 and the second, a little higher up the valley, in 1783. Arkwright's achievements without education, mechanical knowledge or even mechanical experience, are the more remarkable when it is considered that, during the entire period he was seriously afflicted with asthma. He was knighted by King George III when he presented an address to the king as High Sheriff of Derby on 22 December 1786.

George Robertson made a water-colour sketch of Arkwright's mill at Cromford, *c.* 1795. The mill still operates on the same site.

A view of a gas works is perhaps the strangest of all pictures to have been used on a decorative vase and must surely have been a special commission. Again, the clever use of light by Daniel Lucas gives a very good impression of the works (Colour Plate 6). The print on which he based his landscape was taken from Shepherd's *Metropolitan Improvements of London*, 1827, drawn by Thomas Shepherd and engraved by A. McClatchie.

The development of the gas industry began at the end of the eighteenth century. William Murdoch, an engineer who worked for James Watt (the inventor of the steam engine), set up the first experimental plant to light one of Watt's factories in Birmingham in 1795. Frederick Winsor, a German promoter, obtained the first English patent for making gas and on 27 January 1807 the first public demonstration was the lighting of Pall Mall, London. In 1812, Parliament granted a Charter to Winsor founding the Imperial Gas Light and Coke Company. Its special importance as a City Company was therefore recognised and it had a Governor, Deputy Governor and a Court of 18 Directors, with an authorised capital of £250,000.

Watercolour sketch of Arkwright's mill at Cromford, Derbyshire by George Robertson. Courtesy Derby Museum and Art Gallery.

Its franchise included the whole of the then suburbs of London north of the Thames from Pimlico.

The Regent's Canal opened in 1820 and, as it was highly desirable to site a gas works where coal could be delivered by water, this canal became the site for a number of works and additional districts were served with gas. These works, together with those at St Pancras, formed the initial plants of the Imperial Gas Light and Coke Company and were situated at Western Street, Shoreditch on the Regents Canal.

Gas lighting, indeed, must have been one of the wonders of the age at the end of the eighteenth and beginning of the nineteenth century!

Chester Terrace is one of the many terraces designed by John Nash (1752–1835) which surrounded Regent's Park (originally called Marylebone Park). The work was done between 1810 and 1823 when Nash was one of three 'attached' architects directing Royal works.

The view on the vase has been given added interest by the inclusion of figures, a horseman, a dog and a coach in action. The horses' feet indicate movement at some speed without, however, their legs being stretched out together. The two men await their passing, before going on their way.

Daniel Lucas based the view on a print by Shepherd in *Metropolitan Improvements of London*, 1829. It is possible that this vase, and the Gas Works vase based on the same source, might have been commissioned at the same time and even for the same person.

A vase with a view of Chester Terrace, Regent's Park, London, painted by Daniel Lucas, 1845–48. Unmarked.

This piece of rather an odd shape provokes contention as to its function. If it is a night light stand, as has been suggested by a leading firm of auctioneers, it seems a trifle large. Should it be a spill vase, as the writer suggests, it is still a most odd shape! Apart from landscape decoration both floral and bird decoration have been noted on similar pieces. If this shape was in any way typical of late production at Nottingham Road one cannot be surprised that the factory failed in 1848.

Other Nottingham Road Painters

Henry Lark Pratt, Richard Ablott and Edward Prince were among the last apprentices at Nottingham Road, Pratt leaving to work at Mintons about 1830. It is not known when Ablott left but perhaps the best painter, Prince, remained working with Lucas until the closure of the factory in 1848, when he subsequently worked at King Street.

James Rouse Sr, judging from a portrait in the Royal Crown Derby Museum, was not only a fine painter but a fine figure of a man. His years at the three Derby factories, Nottingham Road, King Street and Osmaston Road, strengthened his claim to be the doyen of the Derby ceramic painters. Although often described as a flower painter, he was equally skilful as a portrait and landscape painter.

View of Chester
Night light stand. Painted by Richard Ablott, c. 1825. Mark and description in red.

Painters of the King Street Works

Edward Prince
When the Nottingham Road factory closed down Edward Prince took employment at the King Street Works. His signed landscape of Pembroke Castle in Wales affords the student an opportunity to see a documentary example of this fine painter's work. The similarity between the work of Daniel Lucas and Prince can be seen to advantage here with the clever use of light. The Derby painters all had the advantage in the late eighteenth century of seeing much of the work done by Wright of Derby (1734–99) who was known as 'The Painter of Light'. His influence was especially helpful to the ceramic artist when the heavy oil colours were used at Derby in the nineteenth century and shows how well they managed to avoid the monotony of using only greens and browns in their landscapes.

Pembroke Castle, Wales
Plate painted by Edward Prince at the King Street Works, (c. 1860).

Pembroke Castle lies on the seaward extremity of the peninsula upon which the town of Pembroke stands. The fortress comprised two wards; the outer ward site is now a meadow. In the Inner Ward is the keep, a five-storeyed circular tower 75 feet in height, with a conical stone roof, and a chapel with pointed arches. A room in the inner court is stated to be that in which Henry VII was born. At one time a wooden staircase led from the inner court to a very large cave known as The Wogan. The Castle was severely damaged in 1648 when it was besieged for six weeks by Oliver Cromwell.

Edward Prince has given a very good painter's impression of Newstead Abbey which, to add interest, includes an open barge with figures. A study of such small figure painting may reveal some small difference between Prince and his contemporaries (see Colour Plate 9).

Newstead Abbey, Linby in Nottinghamshire, lies six miles south of Mansfield. It was founded as a Priory of Augustinian Canons between 1165 and 1173. It passed into the Byron family, when in 1539 Henry VIII granted the Priory buildings to Sir John Byron of Colwick. Even whilst he was still in the Navy, Admiral the fifth Lord Byron (1723–98), known as 'foul-weather Jack' or 'Mad Jack' carried out extensive alterations to the house and grounds, but in so doing, heavily overspent himself. When his grandson George Gordon Byron (1788–1824) succeeded to the title, the property had been let, but in 1808 the poet came to live at Newstead. Quickly he gained the reputation of being 'England's greatest poet', but much of the house still remained in a ruinous state till after its purchase in 1818 by Colonel Wildman, who engaged John Shaw to draw up plans for the restoration. In 1931 the estate was sold to Sir Julian Cahn who presented it to the City of Nottingham.

Harry Sampson Hancock

Late nineteenth-century landscape painters included Harry Sampson Hancock, grandson of one of the co-founders of the King Street factory, Sampson Hancock. He carried on the tradition of topographical landscape painting begun at Derby in the eighteenth century, capturing well the beauty of the Derbyshire countryside.

It is important to note that the Stevenson & Hancock mark was relevant only during the years 1859–66. Subsequently the same initials stood for Sampson Hancock.

Duffield Church was dedicated to St Alkmund and although its origin lies in Norman times there is little of that period left in the existing building. It formerly belonged to the college of Newark (see page 38).

The view across the Derwent (see page 39), stated on the reverse to be 'Derby *c.* 1800', depicts the shot tower, built in 1809 by Cox Bros. Ltd, of Derby. The lead was conveyed by mechanical means to the top of the tower, melted and then passed through the sieves of various sizes and cascaded into a cistern of water at the bottom producing lead shot. The tower was demolished in 1931. The fine flower painting reserved on the deep cobalt blue ground border is also by this talented artist.

Harry Sampson Hancock obviously miscalculated the date of the print from which he took his subject. It should more correctly have read *c.* 1810. A plaque of the same subject was painted by the grandfather Sampson Hancock, dated 1835. The Hancock family had been working at the Nottingham Road and King Street factories from the time of Duesbury and their connection was not severed until the death of Harry Sampson Hancock in 1934.

William Edwin Mosley

It is thought probable that William Edwin Mosley drew his own sketches for landscape subjects. He was a very talented painter who worked at both King Street and Osmaston Road factories. The view of Salisbury Cathedral (below) was sketched by Mosley.

Grove House belonged to the Barker family from early in the seventeenth century until 1745. In 1710 the Tudor building was transformed by the Italian craftsmen brought over to decorate Burlington House in Piccadilly and later the great house at Chiswick (see p. 40). It was then that the exterior was covered with stucco and the front portico added. The gardens, including an orangery, were said to be some of the finest in England.

Later in the eighteenth century it was bought by Humphrey Morice who built a capacious Riding School and Stables and who had what was then regarded as an eccentric interest in animals for he sent there – 'All the stray mongrels which

Saucer, with a view of Duffield Church, painted by Harry Sampson Hancock, c. 1920. King Street factory. Mark and description in puce.

happened to follow him in London. Many of his horses enjoyed a luxurious sinecure. The honours shown by Mr Morice to his beasts of burden were only inferior to those which Caligula lavished on his charger'. On his death in 1790 he laid down that all his horses and dogs were to be cared for until they died naturally and the last horses survived until 1815! (*Chiswick* by Warwick Draper, re-published 1973 by Anne Bingley).

A few years ago this early interest in animal welfare was the subject of an illustrated cartoon strip in several newspapers in America.

Grove House suffered the fate of many beautiful houses, and shortly after the above picture was commissioned in 1924, the house was sold and demolished and the estate grounds were used for housing development.

This King Street dish was commissioned by Lt-Col Shipway who died in 1928. He is remembered for having bought Hogarth House for Chiswick, now the Hogarth Museum.

Osmaston Road Factory

At Osmaston Road, the home of Royal Crown Derby, W. N. Statham, Count Holtzendorff, Edwin Trowell and John Porter Wale did much of the earlier work. Later, Cuthbert Gresley of the well-known Derbyshire family of water-colourists, together with W. E. J. Dean and William Edwin Mosley, continued the Derby landscape traditions painting topographical scenes.

View of Derby across the Derwent painted by Harry Sampson Hancock, c. 1925. Mark and description in puce. Courtesy of Royal Crown Derby.

Count Holtzendorff
The service given in 1883 to W. E. Gladstone, the great Liberal leader, is interesting because it shows the work of one of the great painters who were at Osmaston Road. Count Holtzendorff found employment at the factory, together with other painters from Europe, but his landscape work is rarely seen. He is perhaps better known for his figure painting in the Sèvres style.

A view of the Silk Mill with St Ackmund and the Cathedral Church of All Saints in the background is shown on page 41. Another view of the Old Silk Mill (Colour Plate 10) is found on a plaque on which was pasted a faded piece of paper carrying the words 'The Old Silk Mill by A. Clews'. This may have been the name of the painter of the scene or a distant relation of J. & R. Clews, the Staffordshire potters.

The Old Silk Mill, which stood on an island in the River

Grove House, Chiswick
Dish with an oval landscape painted and signed by William Edwin Moseley, 1924. King Street. Mark unknown.

Derwent, was the first to be established in England for the manufacture of silk. The site was leased from Derby Corporation for £8 p.a. and the mill, making use of the power of the river, was built for John Lombe in 1717. The story of how this young Derby mechanic and draughtsman managed to learn the secret of silk throwing from the Italians by bribing two workmen, whom he bought back to England, is fully recorded by him. In 1718 he obtained a patent for his process and was able to reduce the cost far below the price of Italian imported silk. In 1775 this mill employed 200 hands.

Chatsworth House is the Derbyshire home of the Dukes of Devonshire. The first house at Chatsworth was commenced by Sir William Cavendish and his wife Bess of Hardwick in 1552. The fourth Earl (1640–1707), who succeeded his father in 1684, was created Duke ten years later. When he took possession of Chatsworth he decided to modernise the old Elizabethan House. A new South Range (1687–9) was designed by William Talman; later an East front was designed by him and in 1700 the old Elizabethan West front and Gate House was demolished to make way for a new West Range, possibly designed by Sir James Thornhill. Finally the North front designed by Thomas Archer was built (1705–7). Later alterations and additions were carried out by James Paine and Sir Jeffry Wyatville.

The garden and grounds were planned by the first Duke, who did almost as much outdoors as he did to the house. They remained unaltered till 1760, when Capability Brown was called

1 *River Ferg, Forfar*
Yellow ground oval teapot and cover with landscape panels by George Robertson, 1797. Pattern No. 531. Mark and description in blue.

2 *Matlock High Tor, Derbyshire*
On a tureen painted by George Robertson from the lime-green dinner service, pattern No. 321, (c. 1800). Mark and description in blue.

3 *On the Road to Deptford*
Plate from the lime-green dinner service, (c. 1800). Pattern No. 321. Mark and description in blue.

4 *Merrow Common, Surrey*
Plate from the lime-green dinner service, (c. 1800). Pattern No. 321. Mark and description in blue.

5 *Pont-y-Glyn-Diffwys, Corwen, Merioneth*
View on a pair of pots with Besborough, Kilkenny, Ireland on their stands, the paintings by George Robertson. Mark and description in blue.

6 *Gas Works, Regent's Canal, London*
Campana shaped vase (c. 1840) with irregular shaped landscape panel by Daniel Lucas.
Mark: crown over Gothic D in red.

7 *Pickford's Fly Wagon*
Porter mug painted by William Cotton, c. 1815. Red Mark. See page 30.

8 *Willersley Castle, Derbyshire*
Bloor Derby bombé-shaped bough pot and cover, painted with a landscape panel by Daniel Lucas, c. 1825.

9 *Newstead Abbey, Nottingham*
Plaque painted by Edward Prince, 1855–60.

10 *Old Silk Mill, Derby*
Plaque. See page 39.

Old Silk Mill, Derby
Replica plate of the Gladstone service depicting the Old Silk Mill, Derby, painted by Count Holtzendorff with floral reserves by James Rouse, 1883. Derby Crown mark in red. Courtesy Derby Museum & Art Gallery.

Chatsworth, Derbyshire
Royal Crown Derby Talbot-shaped plate with a view of the north front painted by Cuthbert Gresley, 1923. Mark in red.

Chatsworth House, Derbyshire
An enlargement of the view from page 42.

Wolfscote Dale, Derbyshire
Royal Crown Derby Queen's gadrooned plate with a view looking north to Hartington, painted by Michael Crawley, 1972. Red mark.

Watercolour signed and dated by Michael Crawley 1971 of Wolfscote Dale.

in to landscape the grounds and an elegant stone bridge of three arches over the River Derwent was built by James Paine (1762).

Michael Crawley
In 1958 a fine young painter, Michael Crawley, was engaged at Osmaston Road to paint a limited edition of 600 dessert plates, comprising 50 sets with a first series of twelve Derbyshire landscapes depicting the following subjects:

Nether Bridge, Bakewell	Stoney Middleton
Dove Holes	Edale Head
Stanton Moor	Edensor
Lathkil Dale	Haddon Hall
Dovedale	Mill Dale
Beeley Brook	Wolfscote Dale

Byron said of Dovedale 'there are scenes in Derbyshire rivalling those of Switzerland or Greece . . .'. It is, however, the striking contrast between the wooded dales and limestone of the southern part of the Peak District and the exposed high moorland with its unyielding crags, and the bleakness of the northern parts, that visitors remember.

Chee Dale was supposed to be the last stronghold of the once so numerous and dangerous Derbyshire wolf packs. It is claimed that the last wolf was actually slain in Wolfscote Dale, having strayed from his forest cover, in the early eighteenth century.

Painted Landscapes on Worcester Porcelain

by Henry Sandon

The Worcester Porcelain Company was founded in 1751 with fifteen partners, the most celebrated being Dr Wall who died in 1776. The period from 1751–76 is now universally referred to as 'The Dr Wall Period'. The earliest wares were decorated with chinioseries, since the inspiration for home-produced porcelain depended on imitating decoration on Chinese imports.

There followed, after Dr Wall's death, a series of partnerships ending with Flight, Barr & Barr which covered the period from 1813–40, rich in high-quality painted landscapes. In 1786 Robert Chamberlain left the Worcester Company and set up his own decorating establishment and later his own factory on the opposite side of the Cathedral from Dr Wall's Warmstry House site. Chamberlains prospered to such purpose that by 1840 they amalgamated with the original Worcester firm and moved it into their own establishment at Diglis, Worcester, where it has remained to this day.

In 1852, W. H. Kerr and R. W. Binns took over the firm and ran it until Kerr retired in 1862, when it was formed into a limited liability company the Royal Worcester Porcelain Company Limited. A system of dating marks was then introduced, which has since enabled most marked Worcester ware to be given a definite year of manufacture.

Yet another firm, Graingers of Worcester, was formed in 1801 by Thomas Grainger, who had married Robert Chamberlain's daughter, and had a long and distinguished independent existence until it was finally absorbed by the present company in 1889. Likewise, James Hadley set up his own company, James Hadley & Sons Ltd, in 1896 and this was taken over and incorporated in Royal Worcester in 1905. When in the 1750s and 1760s landscapes first began to appear on British porcelains, they were vague copies of Chinese, Japanese or European scenes, often showing figures with a charming background of house, castle, trees, or hills with birds and animals in the foreground.

The pattern books of Dr Wall's factory and the succeeding periods down to Flight, Barr & Barr have not survived, although a number of patterns and order books belonging to their rival factories of Chamberlains and Graingers are still in existence. However, very few artists are named. It was, in fact, not until 1900, that Worcester artists were allowed to sign their work. The Worcester painters were craftsmen in the art of creating beautiful miniatures using prints for their source subjects so that virtually all the landscape decoration used in Worcester came from illustrated books. Two of these original publications, both undated, are still in the possession of the company – *Pictorial Views of the Principal Seats of the Nobility and Gentry in England*

Buildwas Abbey, Shropshire
Jug with fluted tapering body, decorated in deep blue and gold with a view painted in grey monochrome and inscribed on the base 'Buildwas Abbey, Shropshire, the property of W. M. Moseley Esq, 1796' and 'Chamberlains Worcester' in orange.

and Wales by the Most Eminent British Artists with a Description of Each Seat, published by Harrison & Co, of 18 Paternoster Row, London, which contains 'an alphabetical arrangement of 100 views', and *The Copper Plate Magazine*. Others, such as the works of the engraver Middiman, are known to have been used.

Tea services with landscapes were produced at Worcester at an even earlier date. The Chamberlains' order book lists a typical order on 17 December 1792 – 'Mr Will Tomlinson, Preston Lancs; 1 complete set tea china, shanked, different landscapes, 8 guineas'. The reference 'shanked' means the wavy spiral fluted shape of teawares, a shape very popular in the 1780s–1800 period. A complete tea set would comprise a teapot, cover and stand, a slop basin, sugar box and cover, cream jug, spoon tray, 12 tea cups, 12 coffee cups and 12 saucers and two saucer dishes.

As well as tea and dessert services, landscapes were painted on large jugs, mugs and ornamental pieces. A most interesting documentary jug with a painting of Buildwas Abbey, Shropshire appears in Chamberlains' order book on 21 December 1796, where it is recorded under the order of Mr Moseley of Glasshampton as – '1 quart jug, rich blue and gold. View of Buildwas Abbey – 2 gns'.

Buildwas Abbey was founded in 1135 by Roger de Clinton, Bishop of Coventry and Lichfield. It was absorbed into the Cistercian Order in 1147. Since the Dissolution of the Monasteries in 1536, when the abbey was left in ruins, the view has remained virtually unchanged. The scene was commissioned by Mr Moseley because his residence was adjacent to the ruins.

Special landscape commissions of this kind were, however, the exception. Most orders for either tea or desert services with landscape paintings did not specify which particular scenes were required but potential customers might be given a list of great houses from which to choose.

Whitton Place, Hounslow, was a favourite scene for Worcester painters and was about 9 miles from the centre of

Whitton Place, Middlesex
Scene in monochrome on plate (c. 1800) by Chamberlain. Courtesy Dyson Perrins Museum, Worcester.

London. It is interesting to see what *The Copper Plate Magazine* of about 1790–95, which provided the source print for this view, had to say about Whitton Place. It was then the seat of Sir William Chambers, Knight of the Polar Star and Controller General of His Majesty's Work. It was originally the seat of the Duke of Argyll and famous for the completest collection of 'exotics' (plants) then existent in England. Many of the rare plants were later removed and established at other places before the house was finally demolished in about 1847. The kitchen garden is mentioned because it produced, besides 'all necessaries, the finest fruit of most sorts in this climate'. The two characters taking their ease in the garden are probably meant to be Sir William and Lady Chambers. A further depiction of this scene was painted as recently as 1910 by the Royal Worcester painter, Harry Davis, using the same source print that one of his predecessors had used more than 100 years before.

Lincoln and Worcester Cathedrals
Pair of beakers (c. 1800) painted in brown monochrome with elaborate gilt bands.

As well as services, a number of special landscape items were produced, from single drinking beakers to elaborate vases. Beakers were quite commonly produced in the 1780s, the simplest porcelain examples by Chamberlains costing only 5 shillings a pair with monograms initialled in gold, a practice that continued when Worcester started producing mugs instead of beakers. A pair of much more splendidly decorated beakers with fine gilding, is painted with scenes of Lincoln and Worcester cathedrals, which although unmarked are attributed to Chamberlains.

The first landscape on Worcester porcelain which has so far been identified is on a desert dish of the late Dr Wall Period of about 1775, depicting the Hotwells in the Avon Gorge at Bristol, now in the possession of the Bristol Museum. Although the scene is not named on the base its identification is not in question. The dish comes from a dessert service which would have comprised a number of plates and different shaped dishes. It is decorated in the same style as similar pieces from the Worcester service of the period 1770–80. Some of the scenes on the wares of this period may just be highly stylised landscapes although it is possible that some may be based on real places.

The Hotwells of Clifton were developed early in the seventeenth century by the Merchant Venturers. A pump room was built at the base of St Vincent's Rock, the high limestone cliff which towers above the River Avon. By the time Queen Anne came to the throne in 1702 the spa had become very

Hotwells in the Avon Gorge, Bristol Worcester dessert dish (c. 1775). Cobalt blue border, centre panel and surrounding flowers in enamel colours. Courtesy Bristol City Museum.

fashionable and had gained a reputation for curing diabetes and consumption. This popularity continued in Georgian times when fine terraces were built on the heights of Clifton above the river. In the nineteenth century, the spa declined. Today the pump room is no longer to be seen but the Georgian terraces remain as a reminder of the past.

The Chamberlain order books of the 1790s show that many more dessert services were ordered than dinner services. The growing of Oriental and English fruit in hot houses, served to confirm the reason for making the most magnificent of services – the dessert service. It is difficult to appreciate today, when a variety of fruit is so readily available, that its great scarcity in those days would make the fruit course the most conspicuous for any dinner party, and if you were able to produce the fruit from your own hot houses and the ice from your own ice house, it could be most fittingly shown off by the most magnificent and ostentatious dessert service that money could buy. Furthermore, the wear, the heating of the plates, etc, would have made a dinner service of similar quality a considerable luxury with the added hazards of wastage through breakage.

A normal dessert service in those days consisted of 24 plates, one centre, two comport heart-shaped dishes, four square dishes, four shell dishes (an odd shape with a single shell-shaped handle), two melon-shaped dishes, two cream tureens, two stands and two ladles. To this basic set was added a pair of ice pails, covers and liners, although this was an optional extra and not all services would have had ice pails. With the exception of the ladles, all these shapes may be seen in Colour Plate 12.

The ice pails have china liners to provide for insulation and prevent the precious ice from melting too quickly. All great houses had what were called ice houses which were adjacent to lakes where ice stored for use in the summer and autumn months was cut in the winter and removed to the ice house where it was packed with suitable insulating material, such as saw dust.

Cheltenham Spa, Gloucestershire
A 'D' shaped jardiniere (c. 1800), painted in monochrome with a central view of the spa flanked by views of Llangollen, North Wales and Whitton Place, Middlesex, on yellow ground enriched with gilt, with a pierced cover. Inscribed 'Chamberlains Worcester'.

This style of monochrome painting is typical of the period 1790–1810 and some people have difficulty in recognising the difference between monochrome painting and bat printing. However, the use of a strong magnifying glass will solve the problem; the painted scenes have simple, casually painted strokes; the bat printing shows as even lines of dots, rather like a newspaper photograph when magnified. Both the Flight, Barr and Barr, and the Chamberlains factories used bat-printed landscapes although, of course the more expensive pieces were freehand painted.

From present evidence monochrome painting continued to be used on Worcester wares into the early 1800s and it is possible that competition from Derby forced Worcester to adopt colour enamel painting, such as Birnham Wood (Colour Plate 11).

The above illustration shows a fine Chamberlain jardinière, or flower holder, of 'D' shape, painted *en grisaille* (in monochrome colour tones) with a central view of Cheltenham Spa.

Cheltenham became a spa in the eighteenth century and was visited by King George III in 1778 to take the waters. From Cheltenham the King travelled to Worcester to attend the Music Meeting (now called the Three Choirs Festival) and, while there, he visited Flight's factory and awarded the Company the Royal Warrant.

A beautiful painting in colour of Dalkeith House, better known as Dalkeith Place, appears on a crocus pot, attributed to

Dalkeith House, Midlothian, Scotland
A 'D' shaped crocus pot (c. 1800) with a central view in colour of the house, which is also known as the palace, flanked by oval medallions with unidentified Scottish scenes. The pierced cover has three bulb holders.

Chamberlains, of about 1800. Dalkeith House was originally a twelfth-century castle and was rebuilt by the architect Vanburgh around 1700 for the Duchess of Buccleuch, widow of the Duke of Monmouth, who was executed in 1685.

Birnham Wood (Colour Plate 11) is known to most people from Shakespeare's *Macbeth* 'when Birnham Wood shall come to Dunsinane'. The scene might therefore have been intended to have illustrated a Shakespearean setting. A dramatic scene showing a Scotsman losing his bonnet in a thunderstorm, is, however, appropriate to the early nineteenth century. The incident may therefore have happened to a touring artist who made the sketch.

Colour Plate 12 gives some idea of what one of the many magnificent dessert services of the Flight, Barr and Barr period (1813–40) looked like. The centres are all painted in colours with landscapes, with shaped claret borders enclosed by raised gilt scroll work, with gilt beading. Each carries the impressed mark of the factory. It is not possible to describe each piece in this service but the views are as follows:

2 Ice Pails:	Tintern Abbey, Netley Abbey, Barking Abbey Gateway, Essex and Brinkburn Priory, Northumberland
Comport:	Westgate, Winchester, Hampshire (Colour Plate 13)
2 Square Dishes:	Bridge near Dolgelly and Salmon Leap near Leixlip, Co. Kildare

Cottages near Winchester, Hampshire
Scene on shaped dish of Flight Barr & Barr dessert service.

2 Oval Dishes:	Ullswater and Windermere Lakes
2 Shaped Dishes:	Cottages near Winchester and Loch Dar, Co. Wicklow
2 Sucriers:	Roach Abbey, Yorkshire; Coniston Lake; Inn at Buttermere; Warwick
Plates:	Chingford Church, Essex, Bothwell Castle; Clydesdale (ruin); Keswick Lake; Hastings Castle; Duke of Buccleuch's Villa, Richmond; Camber Castle; Winchelsea, Sussex; Lleharden Castle, Pembrokeshire; Brougham Castle, Westmorland; St Vincent's Rock near Clifton, Gloucestershire (Colour Plate 14); Little Malvern Church, Worcestershire; Near Matlock, Derbyshire; The Strand Gate, Winchelsea, Sussex

The service (*c.* 1825) provides an interesting cross-section of landscapes, but there were also some very ordinary views, often described as 'cottages in, at or near' some town. These cottage scenes are usually difficult to pin down but the one near Winchester has been traced. The cottage was at one time a public house called *The Blue Boar*, situated on the old main road from Winchester to Alresford. Because of the steepness of the ascent of St Catherine's Hill, this piece of the road was by-passed by a more gradual ascent and it is possible that the inn then lost its trade and reverted to being a domestic residence. It was reputed to be the oldest house in Winchester but, having fallen into a state of disrepair, has been successfully renovated, using all the original timber-frame construction, the distinctive features of which made possible its identification. This is said to be the place where the incident recorded on the famous epitaph on the tombstone just opposite the main entrance to Winchester Cathedral took place. The epitaph reads

> 'Here sleeps in peace a Hampshire Grenadier
> Who caught his death by drinking cold small beer.
> Soldiers be wise from his unseemly end
> And when ye're hot drink Strong or none at all.'

Many of the scenes can be visited and found to be but little changed nowadays. Typical of these is The Westgate in Winchester, one of the four medieval gateway exits from the City (see Colour Plate 13) – it still stands at the top of the High Street. At one time it was used as a prison for debtors and small time criminals. At another, it was an annexe to the public house *The Plume of Feathers* and, as recently as 1923, the westbound traffic still went through it. The view on the comport gives the impression that the archway is silted up but contemporary prints show that the roadway ran through the gate below what were then the remains of the ruins of the town walls. In other respects, the Westgate appears exactly the same today.

Another scene from this service shows a view of St Vincent's Rock in the Avon Gorge, Bristol (Colour Plate 14) which, although painted nearly 50 years after the scene on the first Worcester landscape dish shown on page 51, is obviously the same place. See also Grainger Lee service (illustrated on page 58).

A plate from another Flight, Barr & Barr dessert service with gilded rim and an apple green border, has a painted centre with a view near Canterbury. The original of this scene may be found in *Select Views in Great Britain* engraved by S. Middiman in an edition published in 1812. It was both drawn and engraved by S. Middiman in 1786, noted as *View near Canterbury* and it was taken on the road about two miles beyond Canterbury leading to Sandwich and Deal. Close by the road, on the side of a hill, a mile from Canterbury, stands St Martin's Church, which is supposed to have been built by the Christians for the Roman soldiery in the second century; it is esteemed one of the oldest structures of its kind now in constant use! The original drawing was made in 1780.

The Chamberlain and Flight factories were the main producers of ceramic landscapes, but the other large Worcester factory, Graingers, was not far behind and produced some fine landscape services.

One fine Grainger service was produced *c.* 1830, and in this case an interesting contrast of great houses mingled with ordinary scenes. Of the original service 18 plates and 12 dishes of three different shapes remain. The pieces have a pale lavender blue border with gilding and the landscapes are mainly of British country houses, some taken from *Jones's Views of the Seats, Mansions, Castles, etc, of Noblemen and Gentlemen in England, Wales, Scotland and Ireland*, forming part of the general series of *Jones Great Britain Illustrated*, 1829. The names of the houses and the then owners are written underneath the pieces. All pieces carry the Grainger Lee mark in script together with the name of the view in red.

The Plates

Weston Hall, Yorkshire – W. Vavasour Esq
Kelmarsh Hall, Northants – W. Hanbury Esq
Wilton House, Wiltshire – Earl of Pembroke & Montgomery
Gaunts House, Dorsetshire – Sir R. C. G. Gynn, Bart
Brownsea Castle, Dorsetshire – Sir C. Chad (Colour Plate 15)
Stackpole Court, Pembrokeshire – I. Campbell, Lord Cawdor

Glanbran, Carmarthenshire – Col Sir S. F. H. Gwynne
Prestwood Hall, Leicestershire – C. J. Packe Esq
The Rookery, Surrey – R. Fuller Esq
Stanford Hall, Nottinghamshire – C. V. Dashwood Esq
Melton Constable, Norfolk – Sir J. H. Astley, Bart
Normanton Park, Rutlandshire – Sir G. Heathcote
Tatton Park, Cheshire – W. Egerton Esq MP, Bart
St Vincent's Rock, Bristol (Colour Plate 14)
Moor Park, Hertfordshire – R. Williams Esq, MP
Wolterton Hall, Norfolk – Earl of Oxford
Dinevar Castle, Carmarthenshire – Lord Dinevar
Wood End, Yorkshire – S. Compton Esq, MP

Shell Dishes
Blenheim, Oxfordshire
Winandermere Lake (Windermere Lake, Westmorland)
Orielton, Pembrokeshire – Sir I. Owen, Bart, MP
Pen Point, Brecknockshire – P. Williams Esq

Oval Dishes
Gloucester House, Malvern
Castle Howard, Wicklow – Col Howard
Mount Bellow, Galway – C. D. Bellow Esq
Hollywell Lodge, Cavan – Lord Cavan

Square Dishes
Blenheim Oxfordshire – Duke of Marlborough
North of Bath
Kimberley Hall, Norfolk – Lord Wodehouse
Denton House, Lincolnshire – Sir W. E. Welby, Bart

Brownsea Island is the largest of the many islands in Poole Harbour, Dorset (Colour Plate 15). It is now a nature reserve and the castle is used by The John Lewis Partnership as a holiday residence for employees.

The view of Weston Hall which stands in a well-wooded estate two miles north-east of Otley in Yorkshire, was taken

Weston Hall (see Colour Plate 16).

11 *Birnham Wood, Dunkeld, Perthshire, Scotland*
Gilded plate (1805) inscribed 'Chamberlains Worcester'.

12 Dessert service of 23 pieces (not all illustrated) showing various coloured landscape views within raised gilt borders against a claret coloured ground. Flight, Barr & Barr, c. 1815–20.

13 *Westgate, Winchester, Hampshire*
Scene on comport of Flight Barr & Barr dessert service.

14 *St Vincent's Rock, Bristol*
Plate showing lime burners at work in the Flight Barr & Barr dessert service.

15 *Brownsea Castle, Dorsetshire*
Grainger Lee dessert plate, pale lavender border and gilding.

16 *Weston Hall, Yorkshire*
Grainger Lee dessert plate, pale lavender border and gilding.

17 *Windsor from the Park. Lake Windermere, Westmorland*
Pair of two handled vases (c. 1820) also showing views of *Junction of the Thames and Kennett* and *Ashstead Park, Surrey*, in continuous painting round each vase. Mark Flight Barr & Barr in script, and London House 1 Coventry Street.

18 *Binstead Cottage, Isle of Wight*
A snake handled vase (c. 1815) with a view of *Muirass Abbey, Killarney* on the reverse and two miniature un-named scenes on the detachable cover. Flight Barr & Barr mark in script, and London House 1 Coventry Street.

19 Worcester painted on a covered vase with snake handles and deep blue ground (1858), Kerr & Binns mark.

20 *Buckingham Palace, London*
Card tray (c. 1838) inscribed 'Chamberlain'. Courtesy Dyson Perrins Museum, Worcester.

View near Canterbury
A plate (c. 1800) with gilded rim and apple green border. Flight Barr & Barr printed and impressed mark.

Gaunts House, Dorset
Scene on plate from Grainger Lee dessert service, with pale lavender border and gilding.

Stackpole Court, Pembrokeshire
Plate showing ornamental waterfowl on the water.

from a print by J. P. Neale published by Jones and Co in 1829 (Colour Plate 16). The house is Tudor, partly rebuilt after a fire in the early eighteenth century. The owner states that the family has been living in this habitation for some 750 years 'having never done anything famous or notorious and seldom having married outside Yorkshire'.

The view of Stackpole Court, Pembrokeshire was painted from a print. A proofcopy in the possession of the present Lord Cawdor, reads 'Drawn by J. P. Neale, engraved by Robert Wallace, London, published March 1st 1822 by J. P. Neale, 16 Bennett Street, Blackfriars Road and Sherwood Neale, Paternoster Road.' The ornamental ducks on the water are interesting because John Campbell, the first Lord Cawdor, who died in 1821 was known to have a collection of ornamental water fowl.

Stackpole Court is the site of an earlier fortified manor, originally built by the de Stackpole family who left with Strongbow for Ireland. The property passed through several different families and in the late seventeenth century was in the ownership of Roger Hart, whose sister Elizabeth married Sir Alexander Campbell of Cawdor in 1689. Roger died young, so Elizabeth's grandson, Pryse, inherited the property. The house depicted on the plate is as it probably looked in about 1810, having been enlarged in 1735. The artificial lake was created in 1799. Stackpole was refaced in Ashlar limestone and greatly added to in the 1830s, and by the end of the nineteenth century the Court was – intentionally according to family tradition – the

(opposite page)
Denton House, Lincolnshire
Square dish from Grainger Lee dessert service. Pale lavender border and gilding.

St Vincent's Rock, Bristol
Plate from Grainger Lee dessert service, with pale lavender border and gilding.

Moor Park, Hertfordshire
Plate, pale lavender border and gilding.

largest house in Wales. After being requisitioned in World War II, the house developed dry rot. The building, which then contained over 150 rooms, was demolished in 1963.

Moor Park was built in 1670 for the ill-fated Duke of Monmouth, one of the illegitimate children of Charles II who, in 1685, led a rebellion against his uncle, James II and was defeated at Sedgemoor, Somerset, and subsequently beheaded on Tower Hill, London.

In 1727, the flanking wings in Palladian style were added to the house by Sir James Thornhill. The grounds were one of the many laid out by Capability Brown. Today, it is used by the Moor Park Golf Club, has two golf courses and the magnificent building is the Club House.

This plate also shows a landscape of this popular scene from slightly different view points.

The vases in Colour Plate 17 which would grace any collection, are examples of the highest quality Worcester ware, with the control of the deep cobalt blue, beautiful potting and proportions, superb gilding with rich deep colour of gold, fine painting and typical pearls around the belly and cover. These pearls were a great speciality of Flight, Barr & Barr, all of them hand-made balls of clay stuck onto the vase and then enamelled over. The entwined snake handles are gilded, as is the flaming bomb finial on the cover and the panels have delicate raised gilding. The scene depicted (see Colour Plate 18) is Binstead

Wyoming on a Flight Barr & Barr inkwell (c. 1835–40).

Cottage on the Isle of Wight, an English country landscape; on the other side of the vase is a scene of Muirass Abbey, Killarney. A later print of Binstead cottage showing the sea in the background appears in a small series of Island Views by George Brannon, dated 1824, where it also states that it was a residence of Mr Edward James. The village of Binstead is near Ryde. This is not the print from which the view was taken, but indicates that it had become a recognised beauty spot.

All the Worcester scenes we have dealt with so far have been British, but a number of Continental scenes were also produced, some illustrating places visited by customers on their Grand Tour. One Flight, Barr & Barr inkwell is painted with an American scene – Wonderful Wyoming – and perhaps more American scenes may eventually be traced. The Valley of Wyoming is in Pennsylvania and covers about twenty-five miles along the Susquehanna, winding from Lackawanna Gap to Nanticoke Gap in the south. The source of this view is a drawing by W. H. Bartlett, engraved by G. K. Richardson, published in London by Geo. Virtue, 26 Ivy Lane, 1838. At the time this valley was famous for its picturesque scenery: now it is a coal-mining centre. This locality was first settled from Connecticut in 1762.

Chamberlains Decorative Tea Wares and Cabaret Cups

It would appear that while Flight, Barr & Barr were making mainly dessert services and decorative ornamental wares,

Guy's Cliffe, Warwickshire
Tea cup (c. 1820) view framed in gilt on a pale lilac ground, with saucer shown below, inscribed 'The Seat of Bertie Greathead Esq, Warwickshire' and 'Chamberlains Worcester'.

(opposite page)
Harlestone, Northamptonshire
Saucer (c. 1820) view in gilt surround on a pale lilac ground. Inscribed 'The Seat of R. Andrews Esq, Northamptonshire' and 'Chamberlains Worcester'.

Hampton Court, Surrey
Tea cup (c. 1820) with a view framed in gilt on a pale lilac ground. Inscribed 'Chamberlains Worcester.

Chamberlains were tending to make rather more tea services, some of them purely ornamental.

A cup and saucer depicts Guy's Cliffe on the cup and Harlestone on the saucer. Guy's Cliffe is near the town of Warwick and takes its name from a certain Earl Guy who, retiring from a life of adventure, built himself a cave home to which he retired in seclusion. The present mansion dates from the early part of the eighteenth century.

Bertie Greathead, the owner of Guy's Cliffe in the days of George III, and George IV, was a poet and dramatist. He spent some years in Florence in the 1780s. He was a great friend of Mrs Sarah Siddons who was a frequent visitor to the house. Greathead's blank verse tragedy – 'The Regent' – was performed at Drury Lane in April 1788 but though supported by John Kemble and Mrs Siddons, was withdrawn after nine nights 'after trying the patience of the public'. Bertie Greathead died at Guy's Cliffe on 16 January 1826.

Harlestone House, which was demolished in 1940, was four miles north-west of Northampton. The house and grounds were greatly altered by the landscape gardener and architect, Humphrey Repton (1725–1818), probably about 1820 when the saucer was painted. Repton is mentioned in Jane Austen's novel *Mansfield Park* and it has been suggested that Harleston House may have been the setting for the novel, published in 1814.

Hampton Court is now one of the great showplaces of this country. Cardinal Wolsey began building this enormous palace early in the sixteenth century and when he fell from power in 1529, Henry VIII took it over as a royal palace, which it remained

HARLESTONE.

HAMPTON - COURT.

Spetchley, Worcestershire
A cabinet cup (c. 1820) with a view of Spetchley Park, framed in gilt and inscribed 'The Seat of Robert Berkeley Esq, Worcestershire' and 'Chamberlains Worcester' and '155 New Bond Street, London'.

until the death of George II in 1760. Five of Henry's wives lived there.

Spetchley Park, Worcester was built for Robert Berkeley by John Tasker, building commencing in 1811 and the design for it was exhibited at the Royal Academy in 1814. It is still a seat of the Berkeley family and has been illustrated on other Worcester ware.

'The Seat of Lord Bathurst' on the cabinet cup and saucer was Cirencester House, rebuilt in 1718 by the first Earl Bathurst on the site of a former Elizabethan house. It stands in Cirencester Park, an extensive deer park with a fine avenue of trees and is still the family seat.

Frogmore House, a royal residence, stands in Windsor Little Park and was originally the property of Queen Charlotte (wife of George III). Later occupants included the Duchess of Kent and the Prince of Wales, and in the grounds stands the Royal Mausoleum erected by Queen Victoria in which the Prince Consort was interred.

Many of these ceramic landscapes are of particular interest in that they sometimes show a particular building in the form in which it was first proposed to build it. Plans are sometimes changed and the final building may differ considerably from the original plan. Such an example is illustrated – a fine Chamberlain card tray, painted with a view of the New Houses of Parliament showing the plan prepared by Sir Charles Barry in 1836 when he won the open competition with his design. It

Cirencester, Gloucestershire
A cabinet cup and saucer (c. 1820) inscribed 'The seat of Earl Bathurst' and 'Chamberlains Worcester' and '155 New Bond Street, London'. View framed in gilt on pale yellow ground.

Frogmore (Windsor) near London
On a cabinet cup by Chamberlain (c. 1825). Courtesy Dyson Perrins Museum, Worcester.

Houses of Parliament, London
A shell encrusted card tray (c. 1837) showing the proposed new building from the River Thames. Inscribed 'Chamberlains Worcester'. Courtesy Dyson Perrins Museums, Worcester.

was not completed for over thirty years and then under the direction of E. M. Barry, the third son of Sir Charles.

Buckingham House was built on the site of Arlington House, a brick and stone mansion which had been bought by George III in 1761 and was the favourite residence of the King and Queen Charlotte. In 1821, when George IV decided to build Buckingham Palace he chose John Nash, planner of Regent Street and Regent's Park to design the new building which was started in 1825 (see Colour Plate 20). There followed a lengthy and disastrously expensive construction period. Nash was eventually dismissed and replaced by Edward Blore, and it is doubtful if the building would ever have been used as a palace if Queen Victoria had not, within a few weeks of her accession, decided to move in. The view depicted shows Nash's 'White Elephant' – the Marble Arch – in its original position as the triumphal entrance to the palace where the Sovereign's flag was flown. In 1850, it was moved to its present position in London, having been built, at fabulous cost, of Italian marble. It will also be noted that the east front of the palace had not then been added.

Wares of yet another Worcester firm are sometimes found – the decorating establishment of George Sparkes, a china saleroom which also decorated wares to client's requirements. The subject most frequently seen on these wares is Witley Court in Worcestershire, the residence of the Dudley family, where the

Witley Court, Worcestershire painted on one of a pair of Chamberlains vases (c. 1840–45).

Dowager Queen Adelaide came to live after the death of her husband, King William IV, in 1837. Sparkes claimed her special patronage. Another firm of outside decorators in Worcester was that of Enoch Doe and George Rogers, who did some landscape views.

This plate shows a view of Witley Court found on a fine pair of vases made by Chamberlains in the early 1840s.

Witley Court was gutted by fire in 1939 and is now a sad ruin. During its heyday in the nineteenth century, it saw some splendid sights such as the great shooting parties attended by the future King Edward VII. There is hope that the Department of the Environment may preserve what remains of the main building and the magnificent Baroque chapel, the fountains by Forsythe and the interesting ice houses and pools in the grounds.

In the mid-nineteenth century, Worcester continued to produce landscapes. The Kerr & Binns partnership (1852–62) produced some fine decorated wares. The covered vase is a good example (see Colour Plate 19). The landscape is a traditional view of Worcester looking downstream with the River Severn flowing under the bridge towards the cathedral. The boats show how important Worcester was as an inland port at that time, when the river was tidal. Variations of this scene can be found on Chamberlain, Flight and especially Grainger wares.

As well as fine painted landscapes, Kerr & Binns were also producing high-quality transfer-printed pieces, especially large

Engravings of Block House and Pittsburgh.

OLD BLOCK HOUSE 1764

PITTSBURGH IN 1817

teacups and saucers and mugs. Many of these were unmarked but all are characterised by strong black prints on ware of fine bone china body and good gilding. The Worcester Royal Porcelain Company still has the original engraved copper plates.

Transfer prints of United States subjects were also produced by the Worcester Royal Porcelain Company in the 1870s, probably to mark the centenary of 1876. These scenes of a Block House of 1764 and a later view of Pittsburgh from the Ohio River in 1817 are taken from the copper plates at Worcester. No actual wares with these views have yet come to light.

The Modern Worcester Artists

It has already been pointed out that early Worcester landscapes were never signed by artists; the Worcester factories did not allow the painters to sign their work. It is most exceptional for any Worcester piece to be signed until about 1900 when the Royal Porcelain Company changed the policy and began to allow artists to sign their names. Even as fine an artist as Charles Baldwyn did not sign his earlier work and it is necessary to recognise the style of painting or subject in order to make a firm ascription.

By 1900 the Worcester specialist artists were signing. These artists specialised in the following subjects:

Baldwyn, Charles	1880–1909	Birds in landscape
Davis, Harry	1898–1967	London scenes and sheep in highland settings.
Johnson, George	*c.*1900–33	Game subjects and exotic birds.
Rushton, Raymond	*c.*1910–53	Country cottages
Stinton, Harry	1896–1963	Highland cattle.
Stinton, James	*c.*1890 (at Graingers)–1951	Pheasants in landscapes.
Stinton, John	1889 (at Graingers)–1938	Cattle and castles.

Biographies and photographs of the fine painters who worked for Worcester in the last hundred years are given in the writer's *Royal Worcester Porcelain from 1862 to the Present day*, 1973.

This plate shows a fine vase, with green ground, painted by Charles Baldwyn with a view of Patty's Farm near Evesham in Worcester.

John Stinton was the grand old man of the Worcester factory, a descendant of many generations of Worcester painters. He lived to the great age of 102 and taught his son, Harry Stinton, to paint Highland cattle and castle subjects.

The ruins of Tantallon Castle occupy a splendid position on the cliff's edge east of North Berwick, commanding a wide view of land and sea. On the east side the building was protected by the cliffs and on the landward side by a series of earth works.

Tantallon Castle, Scotland
Worcester plate (1909).
Painted and signed by 'J. Stinton'.

Patty's Farm, near Evesham, Worcestershire
Worcester vase (1880) painted by C. H. C. Baldwyn. Courtesy Mr Jason Baldwyn.

Trafalgar Square, London
A plate (1926) painted by Harry Davis. Courtesy Worcester Royal Porcelain Company.

Caldey Island, South Wales
A lime green vase (1912) with pierced top, with a view of a ruined church painted by George Johnson.

The castle buildings belong to the latter part of the fourteenth century and the probable builder was the first Earl of Douglas. Its turbulent history was brought to an end, like so many others, by Cromwell's troops under General Monk, who captured it in 1651, 'after a 12 day barrage with a battery of Grenardoes and 6 battering pieces'. It never again functioned as a fortress but was romanticised by Sir Walter Scott in *Marmion*.

Now regarded as the greatest Worcester painter of this century, Harry Davis was responsible for a beautifully atmospheric scene of London in the 1920s. He painted for Worcester for the incredible period of 73 years and his work is fast becoming as collectable as that of his eighteenth-century predecessors.

Trafalgar Square, familiar to all visitors to London, shows the Nelson monument with the National Gallery behind and the church of St Martin-in-the-Fields. Today, there are modern electric light standards, the bus is no longer open on the upper deck, the car would not be a vintage model and traffic fills the road, and the solitary pedestrian would be unwise to saunter on the highway as he does in the scene.

The view of Caldey Island is an example of a Chamberlain style landscape in low tones typical of the work of George Johnson. Caldey, two miles south of Tenby in Wales, has the ruins of two ancient churches, one of which appears in the view, but it is now famous for the Priory which was re-established as a monastery in 1929 by the Benedictine monks.

Worcester artists produce some fine landscapes to this day. Plates painted with English cathedrals, typical English subjects

Warwick Castle, Warwickshire
Plate (1945) painted by R. Rushton, with a view of the castle looking across the River Avon.

such as Anne Hathaway's Cottage, Stratford-on-Avon, and castle subjects are still made, now all signed by the painters. Warwick Castle with a present-day landscape is a typical example. Such pieces are undoubtedly the antiques of the future. The series of cathedral, cottage and castle subjects was designed by Harry Davis and produced by colouring in by hand over a very faint brown print. Such work requires great skill and as scenes are signed it is most interesting to compare the work of different men or women painters. The series includes the cathedrals of Durham, Canterbury, Gloucester, Worcester, Hereford, Ely, Lichfield, Norwich, St Paul's, Salisbury, York, Wells; and the castles of Windsor, Oystermouth, Warwick, Kenilworth, Raglan, Chepstow, Kilchurn, Pembroke, Barnard, Alnwick, Bothwell, Arundel. In addition the series includes cottage scenes in the counties of Worcestershire, Warwickshire and Gloucestershire. Harvington, Ripple, Wick, Mary Arden's House, Elmley, Welford-on-Avon, Little Comberton, Offenham, Cropthorne, Tewkesbury, Anne Hathaway's Cottage and Fladbury are all represented.

Bibliography

The Cult of the Picturesque

Barbier, C. P. *William Gilpin : his Drawings, Theory and Teachings of the Picturesque* (London, 1963)

Burton, A. & P. *The Green Bag Travellers : Britain's First Tourists* (London, 1978)

Macauley, J. *The Gothic Revival, 1745–1845* (Glasgow & London, 1975)

Stroud, D. *Capability Brown* (London, 1950, 1965)

Templeman, W. D. *The Life and Work of William Gilpin* (London, 1939)

Derby Porcelain

Barrett, F. A. *Derby Porcelain* (London, 1971)

Bemrose, W. *Bow, Chelsea and Derby Porcelain* (London, 1898)

Gilhespy, F. B. *Derby Porcelain* (London, 1961, 1965)
Crown Derby Porcelain (London, 1951)

Gilhespy, F. B. & Budd, D. M. *Royal Crown Derby Porcelain* (London, 1964)

Haslem, J. *The Old Derby China Factory* (London, 1876)

Hurlbutt, F. *Old Derby Porcelain and its Artist Workmen* (London, 1925)

Hyam, E. F. *The Early Period of Derby Porcelain* (London, 1926)

John, W. D. *William Billingsley* (London, 1968)

Tapp, W. H. *The Brothers Brewer, 1764–1820* (London, 1932)

Twitchett, J. *The Old Derby Pattern Books* (London, 1971)

Twitchett, J. *Derby Porcelain* (London, 1980)

Twitchett, J. & Bailey, B. *Royal Crown Derby* (London, 1976, 1980)

Williamson, F. *The Derby Pot-Manufactory known as Cockpit Hill* (London, 1931)

Worcester Porcelain

Barrett, F. A. *Worcester Porcelain* (London, 1963, 1966)

Binns, R. W. *Worcester China, 1852–1897* (London, 1897)

Godden, G. A. *Victorian Porcelain* (London, 1961)

Godden, G. A. *Chamberlain Worcester Porcelain* (London, 1982)

Hobson, R. L. *Worcester Porcelain* (London, 1910)

Sandon, H. *The Illustrated Guide to Worcester Porcelain, 1751–1793* (London, 1967, 1980)
Royal Worcester Porcelain from 1862 to the Present Day, (London, 1973, 1978)
Flight & Barr Worcester Porcelain, 1783–1840 (Woodbridge, 1978)

Index

Index of Persons

Index of Places